Photographing
Horses and Other Livestock

Photographing Horses and Other Livestock

THE COMPLETE GUIDE

By Darol Dickinson

NORTHLAND PRESS/FLAGSTAFF, ARIZONA

CONTENTS

ILLUSTRATIONS

PREFACE

AT THE AGE OF SIX, the urge to execute my first oil painting of a horse came upon me while visiting my grandmother. She allowed me to use the oil paints and brushes with which she herself often painted. The paint was applied to a ¼-inch-thick plywood board, which I sanded very smooth. As the horse took shape — well, some parts just were not right. I searched my six-year-old brain for accurate equine anatomy, but it was not there. How I could have used a sharp, clear photograph to refresh my memory and enable me to paint in the hind legs fairly accurately! After much hard concentration, an alternate idea came. I left the unsolved anatomy out altogether, and finished the job by filling the blank space with a large, green bush. Had I painted in the hind legs, the bush would have hidden them from the hocks down.

All through the teenage years, my painting and charcoal drawing of horses continued. In my later teens, the dream of painting the world's greatest horse-flesh captured my mind. As people began to order portraits of their horses, the challenge increased. By the time high school graduation came around, I was several months behind in my orders. But doing a true-to-life portrait in the studio, without the actual horse in view, had its problems. Horse owners were giving me small, poor-quality photos for reference. Many stated that certain features of the old stud were much better than the photographs showed, so I had to rely on my knowledge of horse anatomy to present those parts to best advantage.

As demand for portraits increased, my memory of the structure of living, breathing horses failed, and photography became my only hope. Many artists recommended making sketches for research. This was helpful, and I still do preliminary sketches, but they are very poor on accuracy when compared to a good photo. When doing a horse portrait, the most important goal is a startlingly realistic likeness — and only a close-up photo, correctly taken to show high-lights, shadows, and anatomic detail, can aid in achieving that likeness.

My first camera was of the $12 variety, with a slow shutter speed and a nonadjustable lens. The results left some room for improvement. I was shocked, for one thing, to find that all the running horses came out blurred! With a camera requiring this much investment, I expected better results. It even came with a carrying case!

Now, years later, many thousands of dollars have flowed down the experimental drain in my search for ideal horse photography equipment. An old steer roper once said, "You can catch steers with a two-inch well rope if you have enough skill." The same holds true for photography: skill comes with practice, but good equipment makes it easier. And today's market provides a wide selection of first-rate photo equipment, film, and paper, including many cameras that will accomplish the desired goals when the right approach is used.

After the $12 outfit, I acquired a 35mm camera. This one had a lens adjustable to different light conditions and a 1/2000 second shutter speed, which ended the blurs. When I became involved in selling horse photos as well as oil portraits, I needed a larger, sharper photo for color reproduction on magazine covers, in full page layouts, and on calendars. For this purpose, I bought a Speed Graphic press camera, which produces a 4x5 negative.

This improved photographic equipment not only enabled me to sell many photos, but it gave me more detailed reference material for horse paintings. When I had a full file of sharp research photos on an animal, his anatomy could be mentally refreshed each morning before I proceeded to apply the paint.

The acquisition of good equipment, however, does not necessarily place the end product within easy grasp. I had the fortunate experience of meeting a fine photographer, Bob Hagen, during my senior year in high school. In the months that I shared his photo laboratory and equipment, his influence made me realize the need to practice, practice, and practice some more. Bob and I spent many sleepless nights doing rodeos. We would shoot a two-day rodeo the first day, process the photos all night, then sell the photos at the arena all the next day. We did not get rich from the effort, but considering that photography is a continual process of eliminating one's mistakes, it paid off in that respect.

When my attempt at livestock photography began, I had assumed that the whole horse industry would be flooded with only top photos by the time I learned how. This was not so, and it is not so today. I believe the quality horse population is growing far faster than quality photographers are able to record its superior performances and anatomy. Many greats of the equine world live, gain fame, and die without ever being properly photographed. Their admirers and owners then spend hours over curled-up snapshots, explaining how much better than the photos the horse really was. But I am convinced that championship livestock deserves high-quality work from its photographer.

No thrill is greater than that of accomplishment, especially to accomplish some success at a developed skill. It is not only important to attempt to accomplish something, but to do it with such fervent enthusiasm that success is assured. There is a need to plan to succeed and to pay whatever time, talent, and sweat is necessary to assure not only success but attainment of even higher goals than originally planned. To truly become great in your field, you must constantly strive to surpass yourself and not just the other photographers. For my own personal challenges, the Holy Bible has been the inspiration to get up and try again, to push, then push again, to confidently tread on in a goal of technique improvement, using my God-given abilities, asking for more, expecting and thankfully receiving ideas, then applying them in an effort to do a better job. Claiming perfection would be total folly, but placing it as an unending goal will always be noble. "Do you see a man skillful in his work? He will stand before kings; he will not stand before obscure men." Proverbs 22:29.

Good livestock photography stands out because of its rarity, and no one appreciates a good photo of a good horse more than a top horseman. He knows you cannot promote and market quality animals with photos that are only second-rate. So, if you have the desire to take correct pictures of your own livestock, or to make a profession of photographing horses for others, I believe you will benefit from this book. If you appreciate a fine photo and the planning necessary to trap it, you will enjoy the elusive adventure of capturing the perfect shot. I hope that this book will be a shortcut for you in the journey toward good livestock photography.

In planning the book, I chose the system of organization that I think will be the most useful to both amateurs with little or no photographic experience and to advanced photographers who may want to brush up on technical details. Thus, the early pages explain camera lenses and shutter speeds and outline such preliminary matters as controlling photographic distortion, achieving correct light, and recognizing ideal weather conditions. When these and other basic subjects are covered, the book devotes itself mainly to the actual fieldwork of photographing livestock from various angles and in various situations.

DAROL DICKINSON

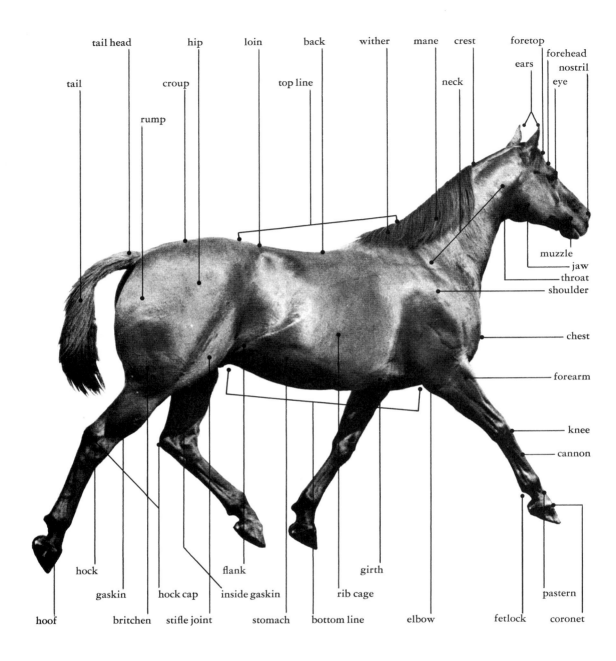

tail head · hip · loin · back · wither · mane · crest · foretop · forehead · nostril · eye · tail · croup · top line · neck · ears · rump · muzzle · jaw · throat · shoulder · chest · forearm · knee · cannon · hock · flank · girth · gaskin · hock cap · inside gaskin · rib cage · pastern · hoof · britchen · stifle joint · stomach · bottom line · elbow · fetlock · coronet

HORSE ANATOMY

xii

WHY PHOTOGRAPH FINE LIVESTOCK?

AT THE PRESENT TIME, over 1,000,000 purebred horses are born in this country each year. A potential Triple Crown winner and thousands of possible Champions may be standing at their mother's side right now. Some of these newborns will be instantly superior and prove a perpetual source of satisfaction and income to the owners, who broadcast their animals' notable qualities through good photos. Sadly, however, thousands of other individuals capable of breed advancement will never have a chance to test their abilities against the well-publicized greats of our day. Because these individuals have been photographed poorly or not at all, the public will never be made aware of their outstanding qualities.

Nothing can be done about the great sires and brood mares of the past that died and are forgotten because they left no accurate conformation photos. But today, thanks to the camera in the hands of dedicated livestock photographers, we can do something to correctly record and preserve for posterity the important horses of our era.

A vast knowledge of bloodlines, conformation faults, and virtues is available to present-day showmen and breeders. The ones who strive to excel in their fields are keen and alert to these facts. It is estimated, however, that over 98 percent of the horses known by name and pedigree have never been viewed in person. Therefore, assuming that this estimate is fairly accurate over the whole horse world, 98 percent of the total public awareness of individual anatomy is a result of good or bad photographs. When no photos are available, a blind guess based on written information is a very poor alternative.

It is one thing to raise a pasture full of colts, and another to create a market for your product. Many livestock producers publicize their stock by first placing an ad in national publications. Then come the inquiries. Most of them follow this pattern:

Dear Sirs:

I saw your ad and I'm interested in your colts. I live in . . . (three states away). Please send me the pedigrees, prices, and a clear photo showing the

1

side, rear, and front view. If they look nice, I will be out to see the horses during my vacation in August. Thank you. I'll look forward to seeing the photos.

Yours truly,
Mr. Average Buyer

Many people never fully answer this buyer's letter; they do not have any photos. They know that photos they might take themselves will be amateurish and may quickly kill a possible deal. Instead, they send prices, a glorified description (pointing out practically no faults), and encourage the inquirer to drive across three states to see the horses and form his own opinion. This buyer possibly wrote a similar letter to several breeders. It stands to reason that the one who can furnish clear and accurate photos along with the written data has a far better chance of making a sale.

Perhaps you will choose to consign your horses to an annual, well-publicized sale. When the prospective buyers receive their copy of the illustrated catalog, they decide which horses they are interested in. Are good photos important here? Only if you want a lot of buyers to attend and a lot of bidders on your consignment.

Are good photos important? The future of your entire operation depends on it!

CAMERA SHUTTER SPEEDS

YOU CAN'T TAKE those all-important, quality photos without adequate equipment and a knowledge of how to use it effectively. Simple cameras, similar to my original $12 outfit with its slow shutter speed and a nonadjustable lens, may be suitable for family snapshots, but usually they are far too limited for first-rate livestock photography.

Much more versatile and flexible is a camera such as a 35 mm rangefinder or single-lens reflex camera that accepts a variety of interchangeable lenses and offers a wide choice of shutter speeds that enable you to capture clearly even the fastest action. Most single-lens reflex cameras have the additional advantage of a preview mechanism that permits the photographer to see how sharp various parts of a scene will appear in the finished photo, a decided asset when you want to fuzz out details that would otherwise take away from the subject.

For unposed horse photography, a shutter speed of under 1/1000 second will result in blurs when the subject moves his ears, tail, or eyes. On posed livestock shots, however, I prefer to use 1/125 to 1/200 second speeds. The slower speeds give enough depth of field — the zone from near to far in which focus is sharp — to bring all parts of the horse into proper focus, yet detracting backgrounds become out of focus to some degree.

At these speeds or slower, unless you are using a tripod, a rock-steady stance and holding position is very important. A hair-trigger camera is helpful. On 35mm cameras, you can shoot at speeds down to ½ second (when poor light conditions justify it) and handhold without blurs, providing your camera is close to the eye and resting on the four holding points of your eyebrow, cheekbone, nose bridge, and hands. This will take some practice before you are steady enough.

A good speed for rodeo and other action shots is no less than 1/750 second. I prefer 1/1000 second for capturing every flying dirt clod, muscle movement, and highlight. At one time, I used a 35mm camera with a 1/2000 second shutter speed, and the results were even sharper than at the 1/1000 speed. Those action shots were so crisp you could count the nails in a fast-moving horse's shoe.

Along with livestock photography, the need often arises to take pictures of ranch facilities (see *Photographing Ranch Facilities,* page 71). Sometimes this requires a shot from the air showing a considerable part of a spread. For aerial photos, use the fastest shutter speed you have. Otherwise, the vibration of the plane or helicopter might blur your efforts.

CAMERA ELEVATION

THE HEIGHT OF THE CAMERA when a picture is taken can dramatically change the subject's appearance in the finished photo. If you are, say, six feet tall and stand straight up with your camera at eye level, you are aiming the camera too high on almost any horse, about on or above a level with his spine. To include the entire animal in the photo, you must tilt the lens downward. At this angle, the upper parts of the horse will appear relatively normal, but the lower parts will be foreshortened. Therefore, if you stand tall, you can make a leggy horse look shorter on his feet. Conversely, holding the camera at ground level makes a stocky horse look taller.

Years ago, nearly all cattle were photographed from a high angle to empha-

Left: *A low camera position, about 18 inches off the ground, causes a horse to appear taller. This effect is good when the subject is slightly overweight. It would be wrong for a horse in correct condition or underweight.*

ght: *A camera elevation of about 5 feet 5 inches was used for this shot. This height is helpful when he subject is underweight and you nt him to look heavier, but would be very wrong on a heavy animal.*

size their compactness (see *Cattle Photography,* page 85). In addition, they were posed standing in 10 to 12 inches of straw to hide their feet and make them look short and heavy. Sometime between then and now, connoisseurs of beef on the hoof decided that cattle had to have sound feet and legs long enough to travel on without hitting high center on an anthill. So today some cattle are photographed from a camera position right on the ground.

No matter which extreme you may prefer, aiming the camera high or from close to the ground, holding it dead center on the middle of the animal's body is my choice.

It was once said that, for a good horse photo, the camera should be positioned so that the horizon crosses the background at the center of the animal's body. This would be all right if you and the horse were on level ground and all the background was level, too. But if you and the horse were on top of a hill or in a hill-surrounded valley, it would be more important to forget the horizon and work, instead, to capture the best horse anatomy.

DEALING WITH DISTORTION

PART OF THE ABILITY to handle a good camera in professional style is learning to cope with photographic distortion. This is the perversion of the photo image that sometimes makes the subject look deformed.

Distortion also occurs in everything we look at with the eye, but the Lord prepared the human brain to compensate for this, minimizing the total effect. In photography, however, it is up to the camera user to figure out ways to compensate for distortion.

All camera lenses distort to a certain degree, but some more than others. A normal lens distorts the least and most closely approximates what you see with the naked eye. It is not the best lens for livestock photography, however. In order to fill the entire picture area with horse, you would have to stand too close to the animal, only about 8 or 10 feet away. This is too near for you to have a good overall view of the situation in a posed shot.

With a wide-angle lens, used at a distance that would include only the horse and not a lot of unnecessary background, distortion is greatly magnified. The part of the subject nearest the camera may appear very large, while the more distant parts are made to seem more distant than they actually are; therefore, they appear unnaturally small.

6

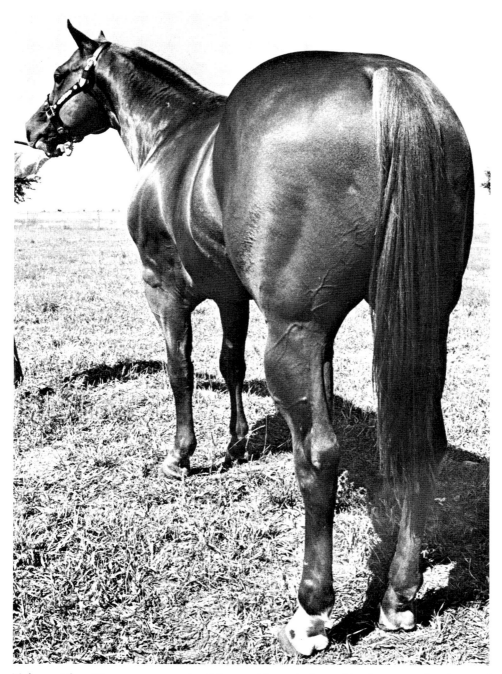

Taken with a 35mm camera and a 24mm wide-angle lens, this shows an abundance of distortion. A little distortion can be good, but a lot is a disaster.

A telephoto lens, on the other hand, tends to bring distant parts closer to the camera so that they appear larger. A 100 or 200mm telephoto is best for posed livestock photos. The 100mm should be used on side and rear views. The 200mm works best for front and head shots. The telephoto allows you to get the proper distance between you and the subject, and the further away you are, the less pronounced is the distorted effect.

To make sure that you and your telephoto lens are at a distance that will minimize distortion, obey these rules. Stand the following distances from the nearest point of the subject and fill your photo with horse and not the surrounding country:

Rear views: 16 feet minimum, 25 feet maximum
Side views: 18 feet minimum, 30 feet maximum
Front views: 25 feet minimum, 60 feet maximum
Head views: 12 feet minimum, 20 feet maximum

Distortion is least pronounced if you move back the maximum distance. This can be awkward, however, because it is harder to see a horse's eyes, ears, and other fine points from further away. You must be continually jumping back and forth to obtain proper shooting angles. At the maximum distance, you have to evaluate your angle quickly and accurately and tell the horse handler the precise moment to freeze the horse into a motionless pose.

In shooting front or rear horse photos, distortion is a real enemy, and especially so if you use a wide-angle lens. Unless you master this foe, your pictures will remain amateurish. A distorted wide-angle front view, for instance, will show a large head, ear, and neck, but small hindquarters. Many horse shots by local newspapers and the average show photographer are front views of award presentations taken with a wide-angle or normal 55mm lens, and nearly all have this failing. The photographer, forgetting the distortion factor, moved in close to the winner in order to get the horse's face and the proud owner and awarding judges. The result is the traditional big-headed horse. Horsemen the world over shudder at the thought of a photo that makes their horse's head look enlarged. Such photos generate few sales of either horses or pictures.

In side views, distortion is also a problem, although here most photogra-

Right: *Poorly-controlled distortion in a telephoto shot can ruin a rear view by increasing the size of the front quarters, especially the head and neck. This tends to take the effect away from a quality hind leg. This was taken with a 140mm telephoto on a 35mm camera.*

8

phers do not worry much about it. If your camera position, in relation to the horse, is closer to the head than to the hindquarters, you will get a slightly enlarged head and a slightly shrunken rear end. The only really safe place to take a side view photo is exactly perpendicular to the horse's spine and not an inch closer to the head than the rear. If the horse swings his head one or two feet closer to the camera, just bending the neck, you must compensate by moving closer to the rear to balance out.

For rear views, distortion can be an aid instead of an enemy. The closer parts can be made to appear larger and the further ones smaller. That is what the horseman likes to see. This makes the stifle, gaskin, and the whole rear quarter extra large. It shrinks the neck, head, and ears. The withers, back, shoulders, and forearm stay normal. If carefully handled, the total effect is a good one. The same lens should be used for rear views as for side views (approximately 100mm on a 35mm camera).

Head shots need an undistorted perspective, and to do this you must judge your distance with special care. If you are too close to the horse's head, the nose will appear more enlarged than the eyes, ears, and neck. Don't expect anyone to purchase such shots. The same lens should be used for head shots as for front views (approximately 200mm on a 35mm camera).

CORRECT LIGHT

PERFECT LIGHT is sunlight, and there is no substitute. Light cannot be artificially created to duplicate or improve upon the great, warm tones of clear sunshine. As proper sunlight reflects from the clean, rich highlights of quality horseflesh and casts soft but bold shadows under powerful, rippling muscles, it is a joy to behold for any horseman and a challenge to the photographer to capture it on film for others to appreciate.

To record this striking play of light and shadow, in an artistic way, is the dream of every livestock photographer. There are many ways to succeed or fail in the attempt.

The best hours for perfect light in summer are from about 30 minutes after

Right: *This shot, made with a 100mm lens on a 35mm camera, and at a greater distance from the subject, shows a correct amount of distortion for a rear view. Two things regulate the distortion: distance from subject and lens length.*

Left: *Perfect light illuminates every square inch of the body. It presents a bold silhouette, bright highlights, and emphasized shadows in muscle creases. It makes it possible to tell the total anatomy story.*

Summer high noon light gives a very poor result. It places dark, distracting shadows under every area of the anatomy that tends to bulge out. This prevents total illumination below the eye, the throat, the front of the ears, and the lower jaw area. The higher light hits strongly only on the top of the subject.

sunrise to two hours before high noon. Wait about two hours after high noon before starting to take pictures again, then work until nearly sunset.

Low light from the early and late sun is my favorite. I avoid the high noon sun because it drops straight down on a horse's back, head, and neck, creating drab shadows all over the chest and under the stomach and stifles. With the sun directly overhead, you also lose the rich glow of the lower sun as it touches the tops of veins. As winter comes, the sun moves far enough south so that low light is available almost all day.

When photographing posed horse shots with relatively low light, don't worry about shadow detail. Just try to make the amount of shadow on the body as small as possible. Some dark shadows create more depth in a photo and allow the highlights to stand out more impressively, but such shadows should be held to a minimum. They can conceal, as well as accentuate, anatomical features.

Your own shadow can help you to determine the correct angle of light on a horse. A good general rule for getting the proper angle is to have your shadow point toward the animal. This will lessen your margin of error but is not meant to advocate that your shadow be in the photo. It should extend only a few feet from you so that, if necessary, it can easily be cropped off the bottom of the finished photo.

When a thin, hazy layer of clouds reduces the sun's brightness, there is a problem. Sometimes a serious deadline is at hand, and there is no time to wait for the very best light. For good black-and-white shots on posed horses, watch the shadows on the ground. If you can see a definite division between light and shadows, you can take acceptable pictures. If only a vague, fuzzy division is visible, you are wasting time trying for superior quality shots. Either wait for sharper shadow lines or settle for less quality. You might, of course, try to fill in light with an artificial light source, but under most daytime conditions, I prefer not to use such lighting (see *Flash Photography,* page 18).

PROPER CONTRAST AND TONES

IN A POSED VIEW of a horse, you are concerned with the two main basics of livestock photography, namely, the animal's silhouette and the body shape as revealed by highlights and shadow tones flowing over the hair coat. Capturing on film the proper contrast between light and shadow, and between the shadow tones themselves, will disclose the greatest amount of the horse's anatomy and

Proper contrast shows every tone from black to white and is very pleasing for reproduction or general viewing.

present it correctly. But without perfect light, it is difficult to achieve the very best contrast and tone quality. In black-and-white photos, however, some adjusting can be done in the darkroom.

For the best black-and-white livestock photos, the tones should run the full range — from pure black to pure white and all the tones in between. A photo with this full tonal range tells as much of the anatomy as can be told. Anything short of this is that much short of being correct. For example, the tones can be too washed out or too dark so that you cannot clearly distinguish one point of an animal's anatomy from another. Either extreme is unsatisfactory. In a high-quality picture, the tones should be in sufficient contrast to make each point of anatomy stand out sharply from the others and from the background. This distinct separation between the parts of the subject makes a photo read loud and strong.

Contrast is the difference in shades between one tone and another lighter

Too much high contrast changes the dark grays to blacks and the light grays to whites. The middle tones that hold the silhouette and muscle tones together are lost.

Top left: A "washed-out" photo is one that has not been exposed or developed properly. The light grays turn to whites, causing the silhouette to be lost. None of the tones have their proper darkness.

Lower left: Low-contrast prints do not show the full tonal scale from white to black. The tones range only from light gray to dark gray, and the result is very flat and lacking in appeal.

or darker one. By normal darkroom procedures, such as the choice of high- or low-contrast printing paper or the practices known as dodging or burning-in, the tones can be controlled. Thus, black-and-white photos can be made to vary from high to low contrast, depending on the effect desired by the photographer. A low-contrast photo is one with medium gray tones dominant. In a high-contrast photo, the medium gray tones have been largely removed and mostly whites and blacks dominate, with a minimum of gray holding them together.

In the case of a black-and-white photo to be used for reproduction, an average newspaper or magazine will lighten the black tones and darken the whites. This is done by screening, a process that involves rephotographing the original photo and breaking the image into many thousands of large and tiny dots so that it can be printed as a halftone. There is a variation in the fineness of the screen used by different publications, and this must be considered when preparing a print for reproduction. The proper contrast for ideal reproduction quality, then, is to slightly exaggerate by making the blacks blacker and the whites whiter.

FLASH PHOTOGRAPHY

LIVESTOCK PHOTOGRAPHY using artificial light sources has never appealed to me as much as shooting under available light. Nevertheless, there is a place and need for artificial light, and in the hands of an imaginative photographer, flash from a flash unit or an electronic strobe light can have almost unlimited uses.

It is always discouraging to be confronted by a thick cloud cover when a busy schedule of horse photography must be met. But if you no longer can depend on the sun, artificial light is your only alternative.

For daytime shooting, a light source attached directly to the camera is not desirable. Its light, aimed straight at the subject, is too flat for good definition and lacks depth. For the best results during the day, have the flash somewhere off to one side of the subject. In this position it will create shadows and highlights that emphasize the ripple of muscles.

The most satisfying use of flash for me has been in photographing light-colored horses, such as grays or palominos, at night. I like a nighttime shot of these animals because during the day, when the background is well-illuminated, it is sometimes hard to capture a bold silhouette of a light-colored horse.

An electronic strobe light connected to the camera and shot at an angle emphasizes muscles. This gives more depth than a flash attached directly to the camera but is no replacement for good, bright sunlight. The strobe can be held part-way between the photographer and the horse to increase the brightness of close range.

To set up this kind of night shot requires some extra effort, but the result will be well worth the trouble. Select a good grassy area, with no lights in the background and no nearby electric wires that might appear in the photo. Park a car with its lights shining on the area and the subject; the car lights will not contribute to the light of the flash, but they enable you to see where you are going and help you to adjust the focus. Then stand your subject properly, and flash away. Some very rich, bold colors will result. When this technique is used to shoot into the last glow of sunset, it produces photos that are unbelievably colorful.

Flash can also be a useful tool in photographing indoor livestock shows and nighttime rodeo events. Flash bulbs or strobe light, if synchronized with your shutter speed (see *Camera Shutter Speeds,* page 2), will stop action because the light duration from an average bulb is 1/250 second and from a strobe light 1/1000 second. However, 1/250 second will stop action only fairly well, and the sharpness of the picture will leave something to be desired.

But be careful how you use flash. A good way to get scalped is to shoot a flash right into a horse's eyes as he makes a sharp turn in a barrel race, blinding

19

the horse at a very crucial moment. Many barrel racers say they have experienced this, and no doubt some photographers have lived to regret it.

WEATHER CONDITIONS

ONCE YOU HAVE a good working knowledge of cameras and recognize the problems that can be encountered in using them, you are ready to get out under the sky and start shooting quality livestock photos.

The first thing you must take into account is the weather. Green grass and no flies is the common desire of every photographer and horse, but ideal weather conditions will also include a bright sun, no clouds or wind, and a temperature of about 72 degrees.

As I pointed out earlier, a thick or thin cloud cover will cause you to lose warm color tones and proper contrast. With bright sunlight, each prominent muscle of your subject will be emphasized by a sun-reflected highlight. These highlights, combined with the correct amount of shadow, give a rounded appearance to the body and other points of conformation.

Even beautiful white, fluffy, fair-weather clouds drifting by at the wrong moment can be a hazard and can even bring the best-planned photo project to a screeching halt. I have seen crews from Hollywood stop shooting a film sequence because of a single cloud in the wrong place at the wrong time, even at the expense of thousands of dollars an hour. It would be wise to follow their example when photographing an important horse.

Wind is considered a terrible problem for the photographer. It is something that demands attention, but it does not necessarily halt shooting. If you have bright sun, and other elements are acceptable, you can work around a certain amount of wind. Horses with roached manes are only affected by wind on their foretop and tail. If a horse has a full mane and you are photographing a side view, for example, put the wind to your back and let the mane lie on the off side of the horse. Some photographers even like a little wind blowing the mane and tail for animation. Wind can also help by making it a little harder for insects as they try to make a landing on your horse.

Heat above the ideal temperature and high humidity can ruin a shooting session because they often cause a horse to become listless. It takes extra-clever ideas to make a horse look bright-eyed and sharp when it feels like taking a nap.

The season for picture taking is as important as the weather conditions on

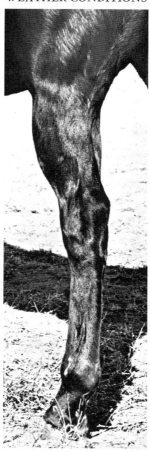

Left: *Cloudy weather prevents a bright highlight from illuminating prominent points and withholds the dark under shadowed areas. This prevents the pronounced rounded effect that bright sunlight gives.*

Center: *Long or otherwise poor hair does not allow veins or muscle tones to be visible. Long winter hair is impossible to shoot through and still obtain good definition.*

Right: *Only when it has a short, slick, glossy hair coat can a horse be photographed to bring out its best conformation.*

a particular day. Because horse photographers take pictures mostly for stud advertising and horse sales, their need for photos often comes at a time of year when ideal weather is not available. Therefore, the season for photographing livestock is a major consideration in setting up a well-planned advertising cam-

21

paign. Suppose, for example, that you are a stallion owner and want to advertise your stud's service in January or February, but you have not taken your photos yet. You have a problem that should have been anticipated in advance. The horse now has winter hair that conceals his anatomy. His long hair covers the veins and prevents good muscle definition. When muscles and veins do not show, you have lost a big part of the battle for sharpness — and probably your chances of arousing the interest of a prospective customer. Those photos should have been taken at a time, usually in summer, when the hair was short, revealing the animal's fine points to best advantage.

SELECTING A SHOOTING AREA

WITH A POSED PHOTO, you are trying to tell the story of a horse's conformation in the clearest possible manner, without extraneous details that might detract from the subject or obscure parts of its anatomy. The more of the story you can tell in one picture, the better job you have done.

Remember, you have two main basics to show in a posed shot: the silhouette and the body shape as revealed by highlights and shadow tones flowing over the hair coat (see *Proper Contrasts and Tones,* page 14). Since the sharpness of the silhouette is regulated chiefly by the choice of background, the rule for selecting an area that will best show off a horse is "nothing is better than anything." In other words, if there is nothing in the background that can run into the silhouette, it cannot destroy the basic anatomic outline. If there is anything that interferes with that outline, your picture will lack the boldness you could have had from a clean, uncluttered background.

Civilization has made it hard to find ideal backgrounds. As more and more horse owners move from the open country to the suburbs, it is virtually impossible to locate an area without electric poles and wires. Critics of horse photography sometimes peer over their glasses and remark that an electric pole appears to be growing out of the horse's back. What they fail to realize is that the photographer had the choice of the pole, a warehouse, or a traffic overpass for a background. So where perfection is not possible, the least of many evils becomes the best.

My favorite area for posed horse photography is a fairly smooth, grassy spot, with as few distracting background elements as possible. The grass should be ½ to 1½ inches tall, just high enough to hide the lower part of a horse's foot

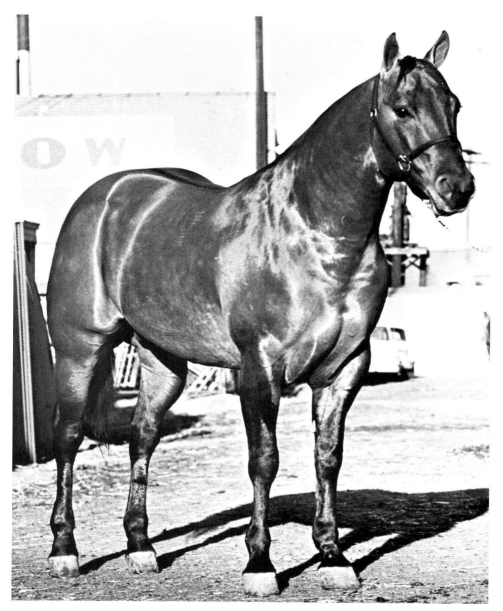

In this photo, taken on the grounds of a major stock show, the busy background destroys the silhouette of the horse. It is almost impossible to determine certain areas of his true anatomy.

When no good area is nearby, the wise thing to do is go elsewhere. This might mean leading the horse half a mile to a more suitable place, as shown here, or having to lead the horse and travel a considerable distance. Whatever extra effort is involved is always worth it. Successful photographers make a habit of doing things others don't like to do.

which, in my opinion, is the least photogenic part of the entire body. Besides, grass this height gives a nice carpet to work on, and if you are shooting color, the green adds color brightness. A photo of a horse standing in grass taller than this causes a horseman to "smell a rat." When you are interested in seeing conformation, and the lower 6 to 8 inches of a horse are buried in grass, you have a right to suspect that some defect is being hidden by the owner or photographer. A horseman who studies soundness of legs truly wants to see the entire leg.

An example of such trickery — although grass was not the concealing agent — occurred some time ago in a magazine ad showing a famous quarter horse entering the stud after a successful racing career. Now an effort was being made to interest breeders in his conformation. The photo, however, portrayed him with racing leg bandages from ankles to knees.

I knew that the photographer of that horse was a professional, so I realized there must have been a reason to hide the legs. My curiosity got the better of me, and I arranged to see the great runner in person. He made a graceful circle at a lope around his paddock, slowed to a trot, then approached me and stopped.

24

My suspicion was true! He had the worst set of ankles and knees I have ever seen on an athlete. As he approached, his leg movement resembled two pretzels on a potter's wheel!

To get back to the subject of shooting areas, the best all-purpose place to photograph a horse is in the middle of a pasture that includes a small, slightly elevated area one to three inches higher than level ground. A completely level area is seldom the most desirable because most horses photograph best with their front quarters about an inch higher than the hind ones. When a horse is so positioned, the loin area and withers rise, the back shortens, and the shoulder slope holds strong. Stand a good horse downhill, and these conformation points appear just the opposite and often fail to compliment other points and especially the top line of the silhouette.

To photograph a horse standing on pavement or a smooth driveway truly reveals the feet and the most anatomy. But this generally proves unsatisfactory

This shows a correct front quarter elevation of about one inch, ideal for photographing most livestock and not extremely noticeable to the viewer.

25

Here the front feet are about one inch lower than the hind. This detracts from many good points of anatomy and does nothing to enhance the horse's overall appearance.

for several reasons. For one thing, only a small percentage of the horse world has correct feet and ankles. Secondly, if a small ¼-inch pebble is under one corner of a foot, a horse is going to look crooked. You may know that leg is perfectly straight, yet the photo will show a twist. If it is difficult to photograph a correct horse on pavement, so much more are the problems of photographing one not-so-correct.

PREPARING THE SUBJECT MENTALLY

ONE REASON you see so many poor photographs in livestock publications is because it often requires almost superhuman patience and painstaking effort to capture a perfect shot.

On any livestock photography job, the task can be divided into two types: an attempt to produce a work of art, or merely a performance. Creating a *work of art* involves the carrying out of a well-planned project in which the elements are controlled in detail and the finer points are mastered to a large degree. A *performance* is an effort to achieve similar results with a hit-or-miss program and under less than favorable conditions, or with the elements completely beyond control. The more elements working against you, as well as inadequate preparation, multiplies the chances against success, and it is only wishful thinking to expect the end product to be a work of art. The outcome of a perfomance is often no more than a lot of perspiration and a photo ranging from fair to poor.

Only a carefully planned approach to controlling as many variables as possible can insure a high percentage of correct pictures. An important part of this advance planning is preparing the horse mentally in order to eliminate discipline problems on photo day.

A horse can be trained to stand and hold a pose, which gives the photographer more "firing" time. How long the horse can stand motionless is often the leading factor in achieving a work of art. Frequently, with an undisciplined animal, the response is to follow the handler as he steps back out of camera range. This act can go on forever, or until the horse is taught to freeze.

To train a horse to freeze and not step forward just as you are about to release the shutter really does not take too much time. Take the horse to an open area similar to the area where the photos will be taken, or better yet, to the actual site if it is convenient. Set him up more or less as he will later be posed. Ease back from him. Quietly step from the left to the right side of his face, always looking him in the eye. When he takes a step forward, give a quick jerk on the nose as a cue to back up, and return him to exactly the same place.

Repeat the quick jerk every time the horse moves from the correct stance. Be consistent. Demand perfect obedience every time. The average intelligent horse will get the message after about 15 brisk jerks, and his stance will begin to be in the desired freeze position for longer periods of time. A horse will often test you about as long as the average spoiled child. The test will last until authority is established.

To discipline a horse, don't pick at him. Be firm, then let him alone. Continual picky discipline annoys a horse and often makes him sulky. Remember, a horse cannot understand English. He may comprehend that a harsh tone is followed by punishment, but commands such as "stand up," "move that foot," "be still," or "quit" do not penetrate. Tell yourself this fact, and save your breath. Train him to do these things by visible signs or physical contact. A horse's vocabulary is limited to a few words like "whoa," and most horses do not understand that very well either.

PREPARING THE SUBJECT PHYSICALLY

THE ANIMAL'S PHYSICAL READINESS, along with proper advance training, plays a decisive part in determining the quality of a horse photo. Many horses must be photographed in less than ideal condition because of health, old age, brood mare shape, or seasonal appearance. Some of these drawbacks cannot be altered. But even with a horse in prime physical condition, advance planning can make improvements in his looks that will enable you to photograph him to the best possible advantage.

Anyone seeing a photo of your horse automatically assumes that the photo is presenting him at his best. You must be sure they are not misled. You cannot, however, expect to make a horse resemble a world-beater in a photo, if his condition makes him look like an also-ran. Therefore, you must prepare his tail, mane, ears, fetlocks, and every other visible part of his anatomy as carefully as you would if you were grooming him to win a World Championship.

Plan well ahead to photograph your horse when his hair coat is at its prime (see *Proper Contrasts and Tones,* page 14). Correct hair is the silkiest, finest, brightest, and shortest that a horse has during the year. This will occur in summer, in most cases, or in seasons when hair coats are carefully protected and groomed. Hair bleached and with split ends is not photogenic because it does not reveal its true color, and it should be considered undesirable.

The muscle condition under the hair discloses the quality of the animal's anatomy. The more fine-line muscle definition showing in a photo the better. This can be achieved by exercising the horse on a systematic daily program. A few minutes just before a photography session, to make his muscles and veins stand out boldly, you can put him on a mechanical exerciser, lunge him on a long rope, or lead him behind a pickup to the area where he is to be photographed.

The belly line can be a critical factor in a horse picture, and this, too, may call for some advance preparation in order to get it right. Some horses are too gaunt to photograph well, and some are too fat. If you want a pudgy horse to appear more lean, don't give him a large portion of hay in the meal preceding photography. If he is too lean, pour the groceries into him before photo time and let him clean up every straw. He will photograph best if he is slightly lean rather than too fat, however. A covering of fat hides muscle and vein definition and tends to make the horse appear soft, which he is. There is no substitute for flesh exactly right, but if it cannot be right, too lean is better than too fat.

When this prominent Appaloosa stallion was being made ready for a photograph, a few unruly hairs were noticed in the middle of his mane. Before the picture was shot, they were pinned down flat against the rest of his mane.

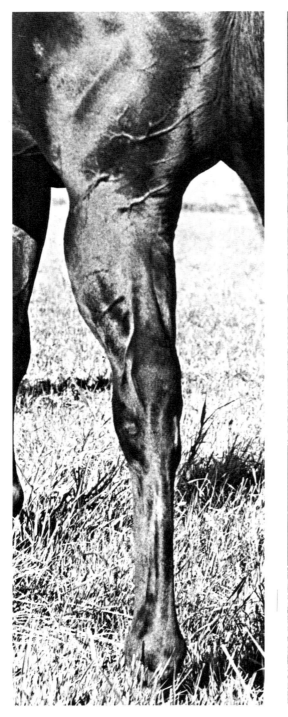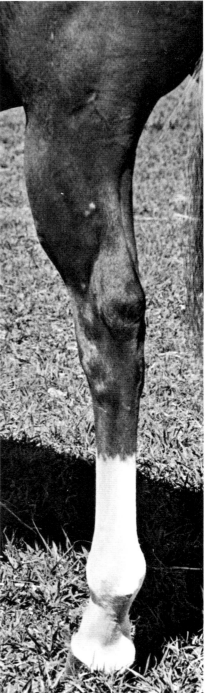

Left: *This animal shows sharp, well-defined muscles. Each surface muscle was easy to capture on film because the horse had been exercised before being photographed.*

Right: *Poor muscle definition gives a soft look, lacking the popping appearance seen in the muscles of powerful athletes. This animal may have the ability to develop, but it just is not shown in this photo.*

Newly shod or trimmed hooves are impressive in a photo because they look neat and refined. Nevertheless, they can create a real problem for the photographer if the farrier got a little too close to the quick or sensitive tissue. The result is a horse that shifts his weight back and forth and cocks an ankle now and then, constantly trying to stand more comfortably. You cannot do much to correct the problem — it is now too late. The best advice is to delay a fresh hoof job until after photography; it may be neat and pretty, but sometimes it is risky. When the horse is posed in grass one or two inches deep, the bottom of the hoof will not show anyway.

If your advance training was effective, your horse should be under good control during photography. But if discipline is needed, curb any urge to whip the animal on the shoulder with a lead strap. A strap welt is often impossible to hide in a photo and tells everyone who sees it that discipline was necessary. If you must use discipline, whip the horse on the side you are not photographing. In the case of an unruly stud, a stomach kick will shape him up.

A good insecticide can be the photographer's and the horse's best friend. Failure to prepare for an insect invasion can cause exhaustion and impatience for all concerned. Some flies are able to endure almost any insecticide, but by trial and error you will find the spray most effective on your particular strain of flies. Certain flies, however, can bite a horse an hour or so before he is sprayed, and the bite will not sting until much later. The horse may move when no fly is around, for the sting of a bite made an hour earlier may feel like that of a newly attached insect. The solution here is to spray the horse about an hour before photography, then freshen up his insecticide when you start to shoot pictures.

THE PHOTOGRAPHY CREW

FOUR PEOPLE familiar with horses are important for a well-planned photo session, and especially if the work is with a stallion. If less than four are avail-

31

able, it does not make the task impossible; it simply reduces the chances of creating a work of art and makes the effort more of a performance.

The team of four should consist of a photographer, handler, foot-mover, and attention-getter. Each has specific duties and limitations.

The photographer should be in overall charge. He directs the program and calls the shots because he is so positioned that he is the only one who can see the actual light angle and leg stances. Using his knowledge of the camera's capabilities for capturing the desired results, he mentally selects the usable poses. What may look great to the handler, foot-mover, or attention-getter, may in fact be a photographic impossibility. In this respect, these three team members must have faith in the photographer.

The handler should be responsible for controlling the subject, and only he should administer any necessary discipline. His main concern is getting the horse to freeze in the desired stationary pose. His worst failure would be to allow the animal to move from a perfect stance.

A handler's proper position is eyeball to eyeball with the horse. When he is not part of the picture, he moves out of camera range, maintaining his hold on the lead strap. If he is to be included in the photo, he should stand in a photogenic position, dividing his attention between the horse and himself in relation to the photographer.

Often, when no foot-mover is available, the handler moves the legs. Sometimes this works, but generally it does not, especially when the hind legs are involved. While the handler is easing around to correct a hind leg stance, the horse often turns his head to see what he is doing or grabs a bite of grass and moves his front legs. For best results, the handler should get the subject standing correctly on as many legs as possible; then the foot-mover takes over to reset incorrect legs.

Actually, when no foot-mover is on the job, it would be better for the attention-getter or photographer to move the feet; the handler can then concentrate on his main duty of maintaining perfect control.

A foot-mover can speed up the program, particularly if he is knowledgeable about correct poses and horse angles. Good foot-movers are confident of their relationship with the horse. They are not quick-moving or noisy, which might frighten the subject and cause him to move. They never assume the handler's prerogative and administer discipline, such as slapping or kicking. The horse needs to trust a foot-mover and not resist, flinch, or shy from his carefully planned advances to place legs and feet. After a few minutes of leg moving, the horse's attitude toward the foot-mover should be relaxed and consistent.

When the photographic crew is shorthanded, it is often easier for the photographer to move the horse's feet into correct position than the handler. When the handler leaves the front halter position, a horse will nearly always grab a bite of grass and then move.

It is important to get some horses to look up as much as possible. On a front view, this causes the chest muscles to tighten. Here a towel and broom are successfully used.

The foot-mover always faces the horse's posterior, and an experienced mover will handle the horse's legs and feet like a professional farrier, gently but with determination. Even the most docile animal should be handled with judgement and understanding.

To move the right front leg, the foot-mover should approach that leg slowly, facing the horse's rear. He raises his right hand to the withers, and with it he gently pushes the horse's weight off the leg as his left hand grips the ankle and raises the foot. As the foot is moved to the desired place, the right hand allows the horse's weight to be shifted back, so that the subject puts full weight on the repositioned right front leg. This gentle but firm replacement method quickly puts the horse in correct position.

To take this shot for a sale catalog cover, several men were used to move the feet, and one person threw a brightly colored blanket into the air to successfully get 14 ears up at the same time. In the final cover shot, only the horses and riders were pictured.

Moving a hind leg is done in basically the same way. In this case, the foot-mover places his hand on the tail head instead of on the withers.

Before he retreats from the photo setting, the foot-mover can easily do any quick grooming necessary, such as removing a little dust with a clean rag, combing down a piece of mane, or tucking in the edges of a bushy tail.

The attention-getter's job is a very scientific one. Unless the horse appears to be wide-awake, animated, and attentive, the true snap and crispness of quality photography is never achieved. No one is impressed with a sleeping horse photo.

To begin with, the attention-getter should evaluate the subject's personality and attitude. A horse in race training, for example, will be a bundle of nerves compared to a ranch gelding used for routine cattle work. The inquisitive young

35

foal will act totally different from a blasé show mare with dozens of public appearances behind her. Each individual personality must be handled in a different manner.

To attract attention with various horse temperaments, the following materials have been used successfully: feed buckets, open umbrellas, balloons, waving blankets, spray from spray cans, rocks in cans, squeaky toys, radios, tape recordings of other horses, grass or dirt thrown in the air, kids running back and forth, crinkling bread wrappers, and so on. The most effective attention-arousers have been human sounds of low volume similar to horses' nickering, or a squeaky sound. These sounds should be made so the horse cannot tell where they come from and will keep searching the horizon for the origin of the sound. Many times, once a sound is identified, interest and curiosity stop, and a different noise must be invented.

A stallion's attention is generally easy to attract with a mare. So that the stallion does not become over-animated, it is important that the mare be used at the greatest workable distance. Often she will be effective 200 to 600 feet away. As the stallion becomes less responsive, the mare can be brought close enough to increase his animation.

Many professional horse showmen shake a lead strap or make gestures in a horse's face at close range to get ears up during a halter class judging. This often works for a couple of minutes while the judge walks by, but it is bad medicine if you want to retain a horse's interest for a one-hour photo session. Generally, this sort of abrupt action annoys a horse, and he quickly becomes irritated. Many times he gets sulky and quits being attentive at all.

Other things that do not help a horse's attitude are pops, boos, bangs, and cracking sounds. He may look once or twice, but there is no real interest for him in these. Often, sudden or harsh sounds will make him move.

Another important thing to remember is to immediately stop any successful attention-getting when a horse moves out of correct position. Wait. When he is back into position, start getting his attention again. Any effective method will soon wear off at a certain point, so it is best to save workable sounds until the horse is in perfect position and the photographer is ready to shoot.

One handicap to the person appointed as attention-getter is the "helpful" volunteer or the interested but careless onlooker. Usually such people sincerely

Right: *The noise of the camera shutter in the hands of this well-meaning but thoughtless onlooker could cause the horse to swing his head out of a carefully posed position. Also, one posterior is enough in any horse photo.*

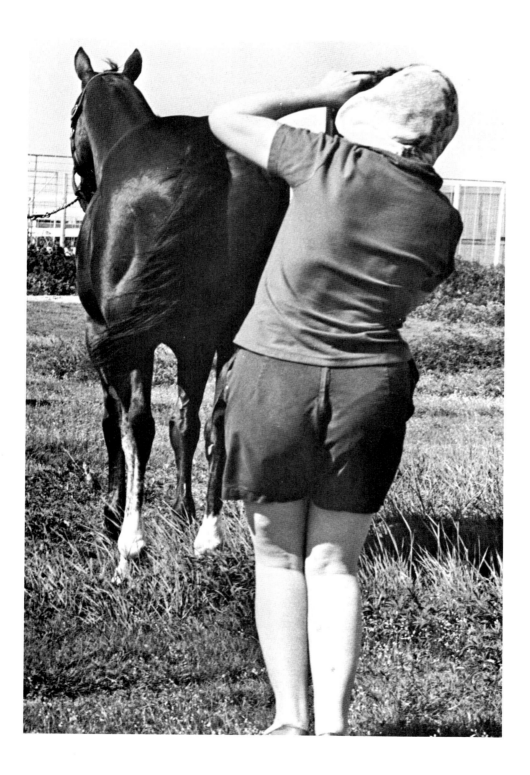

mean to be helpful, but sometimes they are only distracting. For a work of art, it is very important that the horse look in the exact direction most complimentary to his anatomy. As the attention-getter works to achieve this goal, a volunteer in the wrong position or an onlooker snapping a snapshot can quickly disrupt the program. Volunteers and the like, in the wrong place, often cause good shots to escape and be forever lost.

If the official photography crew is in agreement concerning the principles outlined here, many headaches will be eliminated, and a good photo session is coming up!

CORRECT AND INCORRECT HALTERS

IN ANY POSED SHOT of a horse, a halter is generally needed so that the handler can maintain full control of the animal. Because a halter thus becomes clearly visible in most photos, its fit must be as perfect as possible. This is especially true if the picture is a close-up of a horse's head.

For years, I fought it out with ill-fitting halters that destroyed the natural anatomy of a beautiful horse head. The halter patterns used by every major manufacturer had been the same since 1900 and made no concession to changes in the head shape of modern well-bred horses nor to the head conformation of individual animals. The quarter horse head has changed in several dimensions from what it was in 1945. The long-faced, narrow-jawed horse that used to eat oats out of the bottom of a rain barrel and watch every move you made at the same time is no longer in demand, nor does anyone want to photograph him. A stallion or brood mare head, with short, refined muzzle; small ears; large, keen eyes; and a wide, masculine jaw (on a stallion), is now the only acceptable type.

The trail of my efforts to convince halter manufacturers of the need for nondetracting halters was a slow, tedious one. When one attempts an innovation in a well-established custom, the trail is often long and exasperating. I purchased many different halter styles and shapes. The consistent problem was that the jaw area was too small. The throat and cheek straps cut across the jaw and formed a "Y" shape, totally ruining the head design.

As an alternative, I started taking head shots without a halter. This was an improvement because there was nothing to interfere with the head shape. But it could only be done with a horse that was well-trained and stood attentively.

Without a halter, it is difficult to control most horses and keep them from eating grass or moving around. Also, you cannot raise their heads very well, and gentle horses get rather droopy-headed after a while. Removing the halter does make for a high-quality photo and shows off a beautiful head, however — if your horse has a beautiful head to show off.

In the late 1960s, I finally succeeded in getting various halter makers to design patterns for individual horses. One correction after another improved the old styles in one area or another, but did not better them enough overall.

Then, during the 1970 All-American Quarter Horse Congress, I looked over the Schneider Saddlery halter display. Their halters were five years ahead of the times in craftsmanship, yet they followed the same old patterns. I met Stan Schneider and discussed the corrections needed. After exchanging ideas, Schneider agreed to start experimental production on the new pattern I suggested. I was thrilled to think that I finally had a halter in the works that would complement, instead of detract from, a photo of a horse's head. By the time of the 1971 fall Quarter Horse Congress, Schneider had hundreds of new halters made up. The basic pattern could not be patented because we could not patent a measurement correction or prove it to be unique from all others, but the name "Fitted" halter could be copyrighted.

When the much-improved halters were introduced at the Congress, there was a complete sell-out. Since that fall of '71, Schneider Saddlery has manufactured hundreds of different styles and designs using the "Fitted" concept, some of them plain and some decorated with over a thousand dollars worth of silver or gold. Within a few months of their initial appearance, halter manufacturers all over the nation began to make similar halters. Now, the old patterns, with their small jaw areas, are seldom seen where knowledgeable horse people gather. So there is no longer any excuse for photographing a horse with an ill-fitting halter. Some photographers even keep an assortment of "Fitted" halters on hand to use on different horses.

A correct halter fits close to the head. The throat strap falls in the contour of the throat behind the jaw. The nose band sets halfway between the nose and eyes. The cheek strap sets parallel with the nose, approximately halfway between the forehead and the lower jaw silhouette. The nose and cheek straps join in a straight "T" formation. The halter fits snug behind the ears and will not slide back down the neck. In addition to having pleasing eye appeal, the halter must be strong and sturdy.

An excessive amount of lead chain showing along the side of a horse's face certainly does not improve his looks in a photo. Some horsemen cover up a

A correct halter fits close to the head, neatly into the throat contour, close behind the ears, high on the jaw, and is adjustable. Two pounds of silver on a halter does not make a correct fit; it merely proves that the owner can afford two pounds of silver.

small fortune in silver on a halter with 30 cents worth of lead chain. A lead chain should be attached in such a way that it does not cause the halter to hang low on one side and high on the other. Properly, the lead chain should always be attached to the bottom center ring of the halter and be as unnoticeable as possible. Too much chain in a photo implies that strong discipline was necessary, and the more chain that shows, the poorer the horse appears to be trained.

If a halter is correctly designed and adjusted, the horse is ready for the camera, and you can expect some good results.

40

I mentioned earlier that excellent head shots also can be made without a halter, providing you have a well-trained horse. Halterless photos can be taken by several different methods. The hardest and most time-consuming one is to turn the horse loose in a pen and fire away. This is almost hopeless. He moves around, the light will fluctuate, and he will look in the wrong direction 98 percent of the time.

A more acceptable halterless method is for the handler to slip a lead strap or rope down the animal's neck to an area just in front of the shoulders. The head then can be photographed apparently free of any restraint. If the horse moves, the handler can quickly slide the strap or rope up to the small throat area for better control.

Another way is to hold the horse with a bailing wire tied around his throat. This will only succeed on a horse gentle enough to be handled with light restraint; a high percentage of horses are too restive for this to work.

HEAD SHOTS

FOUR VIEWS are fundamental in order to present a horse totally. These are head, rear, side, and front views. I prefer to photograph them in that order. I place head shots first because such photos must show an alert horse to be effective. Some gentle, well-trained subjects soon get bored with a photography session and do not look alive for very long. Once the facial expressions stop, only drowsy head shots will result. If a horse is going to get sleepy, it is better for him to sleep through any other view but a head view.

In a head shot, not all horses appear their best from all angles, any more than all breeds photograph well from every angle. For example, in a breed journal where 90 percent of the photos show only side views, it stands to reason that animals of that particular breed not only do not take good head views, but the front and rear views are not so good, either. Truly superior horses, however, can be photographed from any angle and appear impressive. Nevertheless, before you take a head shot, you should carefully study the conformation of your horse's head to determine from which angle he is most photogenic.

Generally, head views may be taken from three basic angles. These angles are straight profile, full front, and halfway between the two. The halfway-between shot is by far the most popular, although each angle has its advantages over the others, depending on the subject's head conformation.

Left: *The full front angle shows to best advantage a large masculine jaw, small ears, and a wide, symmetrical forehead.*

The side profile is a good angle for horses with clean nose, throat, and muzzle lines.

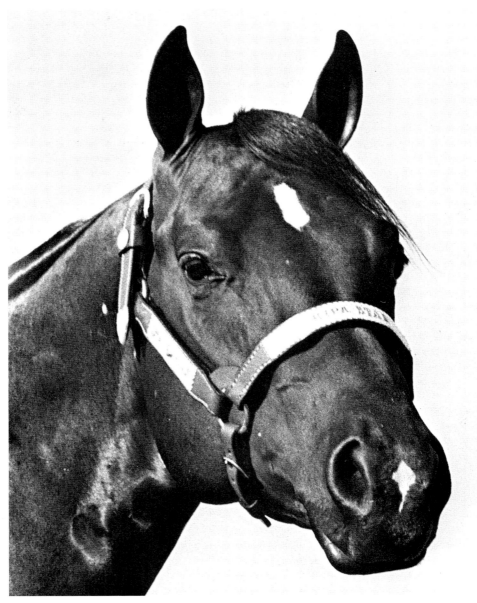

This head angle would be considered halfway between a straight profile and a full front view. Lead chains or other controlling devices should not be visible leading away from the face, and no other background detail should detract from a superior head. Detracting elements can be avoided by background selection or removed by laboratory techniques.

The profile not only shows a side view of the head, but also a clear outline of the underlying skull. If a horse has a refined muzzle, thin throat latch, and a large eye, nostril, and jaw, together with a nose and forehead so smooth you could lay a ruler along them, the profile is the proper angle to photograph. If a horse has narrow-based ears, eyes close together, and flat jaws (as on a stallion), then the profile would also be the best angle.

The full front view is used mostly for a really masculine stud, one with large, wide jaws; short, fox-like ears; wide forehead; large, flaring nostrils; and large, bright eyes. The front view would completely conceal a bold Roman nose, an objectionable dish face, or a fat, thick throat and neck.

The angle halfway between the full front and profile shots reveals the entire head conformation to some degree. It may show less of a great throat or a wide, symmetrical forehead, but it makes up for this deficiency by showing some of everything.

It is particularly important to have clean, uncluttered backgrounds for head shots. There is no excuse for allowing background objects to draw attention away from a beautiful, alert head.

A 200mm lens with a 35mm camera is encouraged for head shots. To keep up with quick movements and constantly changing expressions, a 35mm can rapidly adjust, advance, and refocus.

POSTERIOR SHOTS

THE POSTERIOR or rear view of a horse appears less in livestock publications than other views; yet a well-executed posterior shot can be very graphic, symmetrical, and revealing of major points of anatomy. A man who makes his living on horseback learns to appreciate the parts of the anatomy that horses use to stop, roll back, sprint, or to lunge 20 feet to head a wild cow. This kind of horseman may be less interested in beautiful head shots and more interested in the angles showing the power supply.

Everyone has his favorite angle for his own special reasons. If that angle is not evident in promotion photos, some people will never consider the animal being advertised, perhaps suspecting a weakness in the missing view. An ideal presentation uses three or more photos, showing all the angles.

A correct posterior shot shows all four legs straight up and down and all parallel; legs positioned closer together, or wider at the ground than where they

This photo is an example of a correct posterior shot. It demonstrates the proper pose, with the spacing between the two front legs about the same as between the hind legs, and the spacing equal between the right front leg and the left hind leg. Elevation of the front feet is correct. The photo also shows the proper light angle, contrast and tones, distortion factor, muscle definition, and camera elevation.

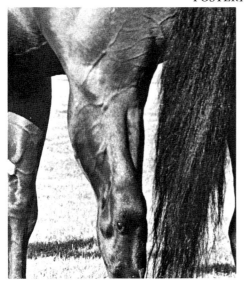 

Left: *One key to the proper angle for emphasizing the utmost in rear shots is the light and shadow relation as it fluctuates around the gaskin. A line of definition should be visible between the sinews connecting the hock cap to the rear quarter and the inside gaskin. This line shows a sharp division between the two points of anatomy.*

Right: *In this photograph, light coming too much from the viewer's left tends to shadow a sharp gaskin definition and also makes the main gaskin silhouette slightly washed out on the left side. This could have been corrected by turning the horse's front quarters about 18 inches to the right, with the hind legs remaining much as they were.*

leave the body, would not be parallel. Each leg should set squarely under the body attachment, and any effort to stand the animal differently for a rear view probably would be done only to conceal faulty anatomy.

For a rear view, you do not actually shoot from directly behind the subject. This angle does not show very much of any animal. A posterior view could more correctly be called a hip shot because it is best taken at an oblique angle, from the hip. It should be shot with the camera aimed directly on an area between the point of the stifle and the tail.

A quality posterior shot from that angle should include the gaskin and all of one hind quarter. It then will show the stifle width, the forearm, knees, shoulder, neck, jaw, ears, and many other major points. A posterior shot reveals a quality or faulty hock but does not reveal a sway back, short hip, calf or buck knees, flat chest, short neck, or Roman nose. No one angle tells all the story of an animal's conformation.

47

Light plays an important part in capturing a correct rear view. One of the main points to watch for is the fluctuation of light on the inside gaskin area. A horse with a good stout hind leg will possess a sharply defined crease between the inside gaskin and the strong sinews attached from the top part of the hock cap to the lower britchen. When darkened slightly by shadow, this crease, sandwiched between two powerful push–pull stress areas, causes the proper highlights to illuminate the muscle structure. When this crease shows prominently, the light is correct for a rear view.

As with side and front views, it is also proper in a rear view to have the horse's front feet on slightly higher ground than the hind ones (see *Selecting a Shooting Area,* page 25). Many times the wither does not show distinctly in rear views. If you are quite a bit to the side of the animal, the wither shows more clearly, and the higher front elevation helps it to stand out prominently. If the front feet are low, it often makes a horse appear to have a poor place to set the saddle.

Shooting rear views can be difficult if a horse has weak points, such as boxy hips, a cresty neck, cow hocks, cap hocks, poor leg muscles, or splay feet. These points should be strong rather than weak for a rear view to be successful.

SIDE VIEW SHOTS

MANY HORSE FANCIERS have long felt that a straight side view, perpendicular to the horse's spine, is the classic angle for portraying any horse. English sportsmen of 300 years ago were pleased with paintings of their favored mounts standing exactly as we stand them today for a side view photo. There is good reason to regard this pose as classic, for it reveals more of a horse's skeletal frame and general balance than any other pose.

This traditionally favorite pose for nearly all breeds shows the legs closest to the camera as nearly vertical. The legs on the far side of the body are placed from 4 to 12 inches up under the body, allowing a clear silhouette of the front and back of all four legs up to the knees or hock joints.

The side view leg placement also does some good things for the silhouette as a whole. By having the front leg closest to the camera slightly forward of the far front leg, you see the maximum in shoulder slope. By placing the hind leg nearest the camera slightly behind the far hind leg, you achieve the maximum in hip length. If the legs on the far side were even with the nearer legs, the horse

48

would appear a bit stretched, and the back would tend to look weaker. Setting the far hind leg slightly under the body tightens the far loin muscle, giving a good back silhouette. Placing the far front leg back under the body causes the upper shoulder muscles to hold up the wither and back, preventing a weak silhouette in both areas.

When old-timers gather and discuss athletic horses, the conversation often drifts to the importance of a short top line and long bottom line. This conformation is often the first thing to catch a horseman's eye. In the judgement of many connoisseurs of great horses, the shorter the area appears between the wither and the hip along the top line — in comparison to the total length of the bottom line from the flank forward to the front elbow — the better balanced the horse is. A well-posed side view shows this balance to the greatest advantage, and the leg position described above accentuates it to the highest degree.

Horses with the following problems will not photograph well from the side: cresty neck, buck knees, extra-straight or crooked hocks, straight or coon-footed pasterns, long or low back, shallow heart girth, straight shoulders, or short, droopy hips. Horses can still take a good side view, however, if they are splay-footed, cow-hocked, bowlegged, weak in leg muscle, box-hipped, flat-chested, or have no inside gaskin. These faults will show up little, if at all, from the side. Which is to say, you can look at a good side view photo of a horse and still not know the full total of his faults.

Normal rules for good light (see *Correct Light,* page 10) apply to side views, with several exceptions. While rear, head, or front views should not be photographed near midday because of deep shadows created by the overhead sun, the side view angle can successfully be shot nearer to high noon than is normally correct. This allowance is due to the flatness of the horse's sides in comparison to the bulging areas visible from other angles. Light shining directly at a horse's side is good, but light shining more toward his front is unacceptable. Light slightly more to a horse's rear is superior to flat sidelighting, however. With the sun slightly to the rear, shoulder, forearm, stifle, britchen, and gaskin muscles are accentuated the very best.

Side views should be taken with approximately a 100mm lens on a 35mm camera. A larger negative size, such as 2¼" x 2¾" or 4" x 5", will give more sharpness.

Any horse that will not photograph well from the side has serious faults. Horses advertised without a side view probably have problems you would not appreciate seeing anyway. If only one photo were to be taken of a horse to record him for posterity, a side view should be the one.

FRONT VIEWS

FRONT VIEW HORSE PHOTOS have been very much overemphasized. You see a large number of them, but few have been taken correctly. Also, a front view shows more of an animal, but reveals less true anatomy, than any other angle. A good front view can be taken and not show a Roman nose, cresty neck, lack of wither, straight shoulder, shallow heart girth, buck or calf knees, sickle hocks, curbed or capped hocks, straight or coon-footed pasterns, or a variety of other poor points. The front view is truly a "fooler" deluxe!

On the other hand, a correctly posed front view has considerable artistic appeal. The beauty of a superior front view immediately attracts the eye of a person who does not even like horses. Because such views show a lot of facial expression and animation, they make striking post cards and magazine covers. They can only be taken properly with a telephoto lens, and at a distance that minimizes distortion (see *Dealing with Distortion,* page 8). The right lens on a 35mm camera would be approximately a 200mm lens.

Front views should be posed just like a rear view, with each leg dropping straight down from the body and all parallel. One of the easiest ways to ruin this shot is to stand the legs very close together, especially the hind legs. This makes the stifle appear narrower than the top of the hip.

A good front view shows the quality of the head, the chest and the V-shaped inside muscle attachment on the forearms; correct, straight legs; the gaskins; and the stifle. And that is about all the anatomical detail you can expect to see clearly in this view.

Like rear views, front views are taken at an oblique angle, and one danger in shooting them is to position the camera too far out to a horse's side. The only way a front view works, on 95 percent of all horses, is if you stand directly out from the closest forearm. A standard view that is especially appealing and symmetrical has the distance equal between each front leg and each back leg. Then the spacing between the front leg closest to the camera and the hind leg furthest from the camera also appears equal. When the space between the front

Right: *One key to knowing when the very best light angle is obtained for a front view pose is to observe the veins on the inner front gaskin. When these veins pick up bright, contrasty light and can be seen winding around the leg, the light is perfect. The further the light follows the veins toward the inside rear gaskin, the better.*

and rear legs appears to be increased, every inch can increase the chances of disaster. As a photographer shifts his position more to the side of the horse, this space appears to double or triple, and the anatomy falls apart. The back gets long, the shoulder straightens, the hip shortens, and the flatness of the forearm and the gaskin closest to the camera become reduced in size in the photo. The 5 percent of all horses that can be successfully photographed from more to one side than normal possess outstanding strength in the areas mentioned above.

If a horse is a little too fat or is short-legged, lowering the camera elevation to about one or two feet from the ground will give him the appearance of more height. If the subject tends to be tall and light on muscle, a camera height of five or six feet will make him look shorter and more muscular (see *Camera Elevation,* page 3).

A good method for determining the correct light angle on front views is to watch the veins on the inside front of the gaskin. If the light hits the top of these veins and makes the gaskin appear round, shoot away. Follow this rule when you can for dramatic results.

THE THREE-QUARTER REAR POSE

THE THREE-QUARTER REAR POSE can be a very flattering one for about 20 percent of good horses. You will not see this view in many livestock publications. Hardly any professional photographers have selected it as their favorite angle, partly because it will not work on many breeds. Only breeds with good heart girth, neck length, shoulder slope, and hip muscle are flattered by this pose.

The three-quarter angle aims directly at the stifle. The stance is generally the same as for a rear view and is photographed from about the same distance as a rear shot (see *Dealing with Distortion,* page 10). This angle, however, puts the camera more toward the side of the horse and shows the shoulder, back, girth, neck, head, and general frame.

Just a little distortion causes the hind quarters to appear slightly larger and the head and neck slightly smaller. The neck length still shows at a maximum due to the straight perpendicular camera angle. A little distortion also can cause a long-backed animal to appear a little shorter and make a horse with a medium hip look outstanding.

An 80 to 100mm lens on a 35mm camera gives the correct distortion factor when the horse image fills the bulk of the negative area. When shot correctly, the three-quarter rear angle can reveal a lot of quality.

The three-quarter rear pose gives a horse the maximum neck length, heart depth, and total hip size, while making the back and head appear extra short. Some distortion improves the chances of success on this pose.

FOAL PHOTOGRAPHY

OFTEN THE NEED ARISES to photograph new foals. There is always a prize mare having her first little one, which stimulates a desire for photos so you can show friends the optimistic result.

Most young foals are not halterbroke. If a haltered foal is leading just a little, it is often worse to use a halter than to let him roam free. Haltered foals frequently will set back and resist so much that they twist and turn into very unnatural positions. If they run free, with no control, their positions will at least be normal. If one leg is a little off, people will still appreciate a photo as being unposed, and as such it has more authority.

If a foal is young enough to stay around his dam, unhaltered shots are not

53 *(Text continued on page 69)*

COLOR PHOTOGRAPHY

FOLLOWING ARE THIRTEEN COLOR EXAMPLES of livestock photographs. They illustrate the suggestions given in this book with regard to lighting, the use of flash, posing horses relative to weather conditions, choice of backgrounds, side and front views, distracting elements in composition, framing with natural surroundings, vertical shots, creating depth, and shooting ranch facilities.

Even more care must be taken when photographing livestock using color film; your film and developing costs are higher than in black-and-white photography, and there are more variables to take into account. In a sense, black-and-white photography is simpler, and therefore it is a good starting point from which to train yourself in the techniques of good composition, agility in operating your camera, and using the appropriate angle to show an animal to its best advantage. When you shoot color film, however, you must in addition make sure that your film registers the true natural colors of the subject. Filters are often necessary to achieve this accuracy. You might also want to experiment with negative and slide color films to discover which one produces a more true-to-life color for your subjects.

Despite the extra degree of effort it requires, color photography is exciting and rewarding to work with. Color adds more information for those who view your photographs as prospective buyers, and it is also more desirable for calendars, magazines, and promotional material for champions and studs.

Shot against a dark night background to emphasize the light-colored horse, this photo shows about as bold a silhouette as it is possible to get. Nighttime use of flash will also produce good side views of some medium-dark animals.

This photo was taken during a 35 mph wind. The mare was posed so that the wind hit directly on the side being photographed. The mane hangs on the off side. Only two signs of wind are evident, on the foretop and the tail.

Right: *A light background with no distracting objects and no confusing lines emphasizes the animal and shows clearly the important conformation.*

Left: *This is a correct front view. It has a soft colorful background that does not detract from the horse. The low evening sun is shooting a rich orange glow on the already colorful blood bay hair coat. No shadows are covering important conformation. The pose, camera elevation, head position, animation, and distortion factor are correct.*

This is a standard side view, which shows more of the total structure of the anatomy than any other angle.

Light coming slightly from the rear puts a dark shadow down the front of the stifle and the chest. It brightens the rear hind quarter and the elbow part of the foreleg. The total effect, giving a more rounded appearance and an added depth to these powerful parts of the horse, is often better than if the light were coming directly from the side.

Right: *Lines directing your eye into the subject command attention. Here a rotten log pulls the eye into the subject and then turns it loose to go in several directions. Sometimes an axe mark on a stump, a square-headed nail in an old fence post, or a dark, stormy cloud can create additional interest and attraction for the viewer.*

Many times a fairly simple, light-colored scene or subject can be glamorized by framing it with darker natural surroundings. I enjoy overhanging tree limbs, foregrounds in dark shadow, or anything that creates a natural frame to add depth and contrast.

Left: Extra effort must be made in arranging vertical shots. Most magazines require a full bleed vertical cover layout. Most calendars are horizontal, and it seems easier to get good horizontals in the West because of the country's vastness.

This is one of the final shots that was selected for the Michigan calendar.

Right: *To create the illusion of depth in a photograph, as many planes as possible should be included. This draws the viewer's eye deep into the picture and causes him to hunt more areas of beauty before or beyond the subject. Here is an example using the foreground grass and then the horsemen, the trees and meadow below them, several series of banks and hills, the river bottom, the rising badlands beyond the river, and finally a distant horizon and the sky dotted with clouds. In this shot, the eye is carried back about 40 miles, and new areas of interest are disclosed on the way.*

64

These ranch facilities were shot from a chartered helicopter, because everything could not be included at ground level. Helicopters are great for such aerial shots. Hundreds of photographs can be taken in half an hour.

Ranch facilities are generally most photogenic from the view the owner sees as he first turns in from the main road. This shot uses a dark tree frame to add richness to the reds, whites, and blues.

Foals not broken to the halter are often easier to photograph without trying to stand them with a halter. Natural, fresh expressions with a lot of poise are a typical result.

too hard to achieve. The handler can lead the mare out to a clean, uncluttered background. Have a proper light angle, wait until the foal strikes a pose, and shoot away. When the foal stands poorly, the handler can lead the mare a few steps until the foal follows and moves into a better position. When the foal is standing well, the mare must be kept as still as possible to enable you to capture a number of good shots.

Older foals that feel independent of mother's protection will walk off and not even pay attention when the dam is being led around. Some of these juveniles want to run in circles and refuse to cooperate. While they are refusing, watch for an unintentional pose, and you might get a striking one. If not, an action shot sometimes serves just as well to show off a foal's potential.

It may take more time than expected, but with patience some very appealing foal shots can be captured this way.

A zoom lens is ideal for foals, because it is hard to know in advance where they will strike a pose and what the angle will be. A 35mm camera with an 85 to 210mm lens is very compatible; in a few seconds it will adjust to fit the need.

HORSE AND RIDER

THE FIRST CONSIDERATION in photographing a horse and rider should be the horse's conformation. If the horse appears weak at a certain angle, that angle should be avoided. Most horses have an angle that is best for them. To capitalize on that angle is always advantageous in mounted shots.

A front view is the choice of many horsemen. This shows the front of both horse and rider, as well as the front part of the tack. In setting up front shots, the same methods should be used as for posed horses without a rider.

The rider should concentrate on the horse remaining stationary. A rider is limited in helping to set up the pose because he cannot see where the legs are. It is therefore nearly impossible for him to move the horse back and forth to obtain the proper leg positions. The photographer can do a better job than the rider because he can see the full picture and move the legs accordingly. It is much more convenient, however, if a third party can be on hand to stand the horse correctly.

A side view also makes a good mounted shot. Although it shows more horse and tack than a front view, this angle is generally not favored over the front

69

This represents the most popular pose and angle for horse-and-rider shots.

view. The mounted side view should be set up in the same manner as a side view without a rider.

A variety of other good angles can be taken of close-up poses, but if the camera is too close to the rider and must be aimed slightly upward, it can emphasize the distortion factor (see *Dealing with Distortion,* page 8). Therefore, a 200mm telephoto lens should be used at an appropriate distance for close-ups and for any other mounted shots involving front views, even though the view may only include the horse's head and the rider from the knees up.

Any posed, mounted view should be photographed 6 to 10 times to make sure of one superior shot. Every shot may look good to the camera's eye, but it always pays to take a few extras for insurance.

CATTLE PHOTOGRAPHY

ABOUT 20 YEARS AGO, you could leaf through any cattle magazine and see only one kind of cattle photo. Every one of them showed the same pose, leg position, and three-quarter front view angle. The procedure used to take this shot was fake from the word "go."

I once watched a famous cattle photographer of that day as he performed his act. Step one was to dig a hole about a foot deep and three feet across and smooth out the sides to a gentle slope so the hole would not be too apparent. He then sprinkled several bales of fluffy, yellow straw a foot or so deep all over the area to further conceal the true ground level. Finally, he set up a false backdrop. His scene was now ready.

A bull was led up and its hind feet pushed into the hole, while the front feet remained on level ground. The bull was posed with a square leg stance for the three-quarter front view. Because of the unnatural, sloping angle of the animal's back, the camera had to be mounted on a six-foot tripod to zero in correctly. The false back angle made the hindquarters appear to stretch backward, increasing the appearance of a full, plump, round hindquarter. The fluffy hay also made the legs appear a foot shorter. The total image was a very round blob of fat with a little meat under the fat.

To add to the deceit, the back line was retouched in the finished photo to make it look perfectly straight. The hindquarter was also retouched to seem still larger, and a better-looking false tail was drawn in.

This dishonest procedure went on and on. Cattlemen knew how these photos

This Beefmaster bull was photographed in range condition, without halter. He was led with an enticement of feed until his leg position was correct. Correct light shows his extremely muscular qualities.

were taken, but the majority accepted the final results. They apparently figured that the only way to have a photo better than the competition's was to put up with the faking and do more retouching. So photographers, capitalizing on the popular belief that "photos don't lie," lied to the entire cattle-raising world for years.

In the early 1960s, the Lasater Ranch of Colorado began using the caption under its Beefmaster advertisements, "Unretouched range photo by Darol Dickinson." Readers then knew such a photo was an honest mechanical reproduction showing an ungroomed bovine in pasture condition. The ads were valid and revealed the true conformation of a real animal. After these ads started to appear, little by little the cattle industry began to realize that an honest portrayal was the most acceptable.

Good cattle photos feature angles that emphasize the highest quality cuts of meat. This means mostly side views rather than front views, and shots taken from slightly to the rear. Today, nearly all photos in cattle magazines show side views, many of them taken in pastures, and there are fewer photos in which such cover-up methods as retouching, excessive clipping, and grooming are used. The cattleman now wants to see a true picture and no longer appreciates anything less.

Cattle should be photographed basically the same as horses. The camera should be positioned about six inches lower on most cattle because they are about one foot shorter in height.

Pasture photography of cattle roaming loose can be as frustrating as photographing free-running foals, but with patience, some beautiful shots can result. A massive animal shown in a pasture setting, with no distracting background material and with correct light, is very much appreciated as a work of art. To capture a correct halterless pose of a superior bovine is a challenge and a thrill.

For such shots, the help of a good herdsman with a feed bucket is of great value. He can encourage the subject to follow him with feed cubes, or even to step up to him if the animal is gentle enough. A feed bucket held high in the air will generally raise the head angle for a good alert appearance. When the animal strikes a flattering stance with proper light, start shooting.

An 80 to 210mm zoom lens with a 35mm camera works best for cattle. When following an old bull all over the pasture, it is a pleasure to have light equipment.

Each breed of cattle has special traits. The best photo of each breed presents that breed at its best. To photograph a Texas Longhorn, the same rules apply as for a side view of a horse. One special addition to the rules for Longhorns is to be sure to get the animal looking directly at you in order to show the entire horn spread.

ACTION!

THE FIRST PRINCIPLE for action shots is, "be ready." No true photographer carries an unloaded camera to a rodeo or other site of real or possible action, any more than an elephant hunter carries an unloaded rifle. Always have the camera ready and set with approximate lens opening and shutter speed. Even if you are not set correctly and some wild thing happens, take a chance and shoot anyway. Some of the wildest and most unusual shots are taken with barely a second's notice. The experienced photographer grabs a camera and shoots rapidly, while others drop their mouths open and simply watch the sudden explosion of action.

Sharp photos are a major consideration with action. To properly stop a horse's flying feet so that you can clearly see the shoe nails is the pride of any photographer. A shutter speed of 1/1000 second or faster is fast enough with any lens — normal, wide-angle, telephoto, or zoom. Good focus for sharpness, however, is not always possible as subjects run toward or away from the camera. Many times, a good guess as to where the action will go is the best you can do. The better guessers get the sharpest photos. If you cannot focus fast enough to catch a critical point in an action, the use of films with faster ASA ratings sometimes gives greater depth of field; unfortunately, fast films produce grainy photos. Each person must evaluate his own ability for fast focusing and then decide on the amount of graininess that is acceptable.

The following methods are for photographing many normal rodeo and other horse-related events in daylight. Unless otherwise instructed, use an 80 to 210mm zoom telephoto lens for best results. The same light-rules hold for most good action shots as for posed livestock photos. Your arena position should be chosen in relation to the sun's illumination. Backlighting — light coming from behind the subject and toward you — gives a good silhouette but does nothing for muscle definition or facial expressions, leaving them shadowed.

All action shots should be taken at the perfect "peak of action." By this, I mean the climax of a performance, the moment when the action is at its very highest.

No matter what event you are photographing, make every effort to cooperate with the show management and the contestants. Special care should be taken to make sure you do not scare someone's mount and cause the rider to place out of the ribbons. An act of this nature could be unforgivable to some horsemen and prove a real detriment to serious action photography.

Good barrel racing photos show speed, sharp action, excellent form, muscles powerfully moving, and a generally controlled look.

Barrel Racing. For this rodeo event, you should be standing straight up with the camera at eye level or higher, like from the top of an arena fence. This elevation makes the horse's turning at a barrel appear as low as possible and also gives an evaluation of the horse's coordination and speed and the rider's form. With a horse coming toward the camera, this high angle causes the animal's head to appear lower and more controlled.

A low camera elevation may show superior action, but generally, low-angle photos are not favored by the barrel racers. The low elevation causes the horse to appear higher off the ground and may even make the rider look higher in the saddle. This might make good sports reporting, but the contestants do not appreciate it.

Cutting. The camera elevation should be the same as for good barrel racing shots, for the same reasons. Cutting horses also should be photographed turning low to the ground, with their heads low. The best shots usually are taken just as the horse is completing a turn and begins to turn away from the camera. An ideal place to shoot is from a position as directly in front of the horse as possible. Your chosen arena position may not enable you to stand at an ideal spot, however. In that case, a position near the arena fence will have to do. Sometimes in cutting, the turn-back riders become the cause of many lost shots.

Experienced photographers approach cutting action shots in different ways. Some wait until the fantastic run and turn, then carefully try to capture the highlight of the action. Others blast away, taking perhaps 10 to 20 shots per minute and hoping that at least one will catch the action at its peak. Your decision on how to shoot will be determined by the cost of film versus the possibility for photo sales and by your reflexes for accurate timing.

Steer Roping. Your arena position is of prime importance for heading and heeling photos. It is difficult, however, to locate the correct shooting spot for this event. The center of the arena is great, providing the arena is private or for practice roping. Second best, in a public arena with a show going on, would be along either side of the arena fence and opposite the arena center.

A telephoto zoom lens is very helpful for steer roping because the action can quickly shift from being very widespread to being tight or distant. Camera elevation is not critical for this event.

My favorite format for steer-roping photos is a vertical one. With this format, as the action approaches you, you can line it up from distant to close and fill the entire photo frame with intense activity. Also, as the rope is thrown toward you it appears very short. The angle to avoid is a horizontal shot, perpendicular to the action. This would show long stretches of rope against unimportant background and force the horses, riders and steer to become only small figures in the photo.

Several points of high action can be captured in steer roping. First is the throw, as the rope snakes out toward or around the steer's horns. If the roper often misses, or the horse is slow and chases the steer to the far arena fence, take this shot anyway; it is all you will get of that particular roping attempt. Second is the moment when the steer is turned as the heeler comes in to rope the heels. The third high action point is the heeler's throw, showing the loop being laid in front of the steer's hind legs. The final high point is the stretch at the head and heel'n climax.

Calf Roping. The shot that captures the top style of the fast roper is the front-view jerk shot. This shows the calf being jerked high in the air by the rope, with the rider dismounting just as the horse finishes a sudden stop. Every top roper gets chills up his back at the thought of a good photo showing his best performance.

A zoom lens is great for steer roping, because the action is coming and going from a wide to a narrow format. I prefer vertical shots in this event. They make it easier to fill the photo area with wall-to-wall picture.

A very low camera elevation improves the angle on the calf and emphasizes the height of the animal when jerked. Other calf-roping shots need not be taken from an especially low elevation.

Reining. Several parts of a normal reining pattern, if they are ridden in top form, make excellent photos. The stop is the crowning point in a good reining run. Unless a horse stops correctly, at good speed, his odds of winning the event are poor. The stop, therefore, is the place to get those first-rate shots. Several

This calf roping shot shows the slack being jerked at the very peak of action. A tenth of a second sooner or later would have totally missed this peak. Every act in rodeo or horse show events has a climactic point, which should be diligently sought and captured on film.

problems arise at this point, however. First, each horse stops with a slightly different style. One drops low to the ground as he slides to the stop, then comes up as he reaches the stop itself, while another gets lower in the sliding position just before completing the stop. Secondly, some horses tend to raise their heads higher earlier in the stop than further into it. Thirdly, some horses bounce a little during a stop and strike several poses, either good or bad for photos.

To solve these problems, only two things can be done. Acquaint yourself with reining patterns and, if possible, know beforehand how the horse and rider perform. Otherwise, get as many shots as you can, and hope you will beat the odds.

Rollbacks and spins make good action shots. Again, take several. Many

The sliding stop is the outstanding part of a good reining event. It should appear controlled, fast, and humane. Proper light on the horse's muscles will make them stand out to best advantage.

---

things showing poor form will appear in a photo that a judge cannot see during the action, such as awkward leg positions, riders out of balance, or horses' heads high and their mouths open.

Pictures can easily be taken during the circles and figure eights, but these are generally not appreciated by the riders because they do not show any particularly hard maneuvers to be proud of.

Bucking Events. These are much easier to shoot now than they were before quality telephoto lenses were generally available. When I used to work rodeos with Bob Hagen for a living, the good photographers were the ones who got right down in front of the bucking bulls or horses for close-ups. For these events, the photographer had to be as fleet-footed as he was trigger-fingered.

This rodeo shot shows how a strobe light, synchronized with a 1/1000 second shutter speed, stops flying drops of water as this bull performs in a foot of flash flood water.

Today, with the convenience of a telephoto zoom lens, a photographer can snap such shots from behind the protection of the arena fence and at a distance of from 50 to 200 feet. A lot more thought can go into an action shot made this way than with a ton of Brahman bull tearing up the arena 15 feet away from you.

A good bucking ride gives enough time for several shots. If you anticipate a short, sudden ending to the cowboy's efforts to stay aboard, don't wait long to start shooting. Get off a quick shot on the first jump, for the show may end right there. Many famous bucking photos have been taken on the first jump out of the chute.

Traditionally, the local press has loved to shoot rodeo bucking events with some poor cowboy getting spun into orbit, with a horn or hoof perilously close to, or in, his back. They enjoy printing these shots to dramatize the wild and woolly American sport of rodeo. But don't try to sell such photos to the rodeo contestants. They have receipts from surgeons — enough to recall those literally high points of their lives. They want, instead, a shot showing class and style in a high-scoring, hard-spurring ride that brings home some day money.

Jumping. Like all good action photos, jumping shots should be captured at the very peak of action to show the rider's top form and the horse's highest jumping ability. Anything less than this will be a disappointment to both photographer and rider.

The preferred angle for a jumping shot is somewhere between a front and a side view. The effect of height can be emphasized to the fullest by a very low camera elevation. This allows the photographer to shoot up at the action. The low angle also gives a sky background instead of a cluttered arena. Dirt should show at the bottom of this shot to indicate how far off the ground the jumper is. A normal lens, rather than a telephoto lens, captures the effect of height best. You can only use it, however, if the show manager will permit you into the arena for a close-up.

Pleasure Classes. Pleasure class events do not offer a lot of variety for photographers. You have riders on the rail at different gaits, and it is just a matter of catching them when they are not bouncing or out of position. The set of the horse's head should be correct for any particular gait. Sometimes, photos of a horse's legs in a poor position can make the horse look really bad. By taking several shots, the odds of catching a good leg position multiply with each shot. Only a very skilled photographer can effectively catch moving legs in a planned position. It costs film to do this, but several frames of film are a small investment compared to the value of a good photo.

Proper light is a must for pleasure class shots. A standing position in the arena center is the best angle for the shot. Be sure to ask permission to enter the arena.

CROWD PRESSURE

CROWD PRESSURE is something you must learn to cope with, whether you are photographing a crowded spectacle like a rodeo or a major horse show, or a single horse before a large audience. How well you manage to overcome it will, to some degree, influence your success.

Crowd pressure — or stage fright or whatever you want to call it — is the fear of failure encouraged by the thought that a large number of spectators may be wondering if you know what you are doing. It is a real thing, and it affects not only photographers, but many people in other professional skills, from a top bull rider to a politician or an actor.

One not uncommon example of the affect of crowd pressure on an otherwise competent person is the judge of a large horse show, a well-known horseman whose decisions out behind the barn are faultless regarding training and breeding. But at show time, this respected horseman walks into the arena before thousands of eyes and makes some unbelievably foolish decisions. Is he actually a poor horseman? Has he been bought off? Absolutely not! He just cannot cope with crowd pressure.

This also applies to photographers who are not yet professionals but are anxious to prove their talent. Years ago I knew a sales manager who sometimes did livestock photography as a sideline. He said that once he was shooting a really top horse, with many prominent horsemen watching. In an effort to impress the audience with his photographic ability and performance, he quickly shot roll after roll, jumping in every direction as he fired the shutter time after time. The horsemen were impressed by his athletic ability, but when the photos were processed, the results were disappointing.

The proper attitude toward a crowd is to totally ignore it, as though it did not exist. Only good photos are sellable, and you cannot take them if you are worrying about what others might think. In the first place, from the onlookers' vantage point, they probably cannot see accurately the fine points of positioning a horse correctly. In the second place, if you take some extra time to get the horse in correct position, they will assume that you know your business. In 10 years, the crowd will have forgotten the extra minutes, but in the meanwhile you have made your reputation as a livestock photographer.

Remember, then, when a job of photography needs doing, check your film and camera settings prior to shooting and concentrate only on obtaining superior results. At the same time, keep in mind that a horse handler cannot always tell how well or badly a horse is standing. He must depend on you to tell him which way to move the horse. The photographer is in charge, not the crowd.

COVER-QUALITY PHOTOS

THE JOY AND SATISFACTION of planning and capturing a beautiful, cover- or calendar-quality color shot is rewarding for any dedicated photographer. Many editors and readers of livestock publications as well as calendar fanciers never dream of the total effort involved. To create a photographic masterpiece of this kind calls for the expert blending of many factors, including time, light, manpower, subject, and nature itself.

This behind-the-scenes shot shows preparations for the Michigan calendar photograph (see page 64), with the tree limb positioned to form a frame above the horses.

The first consideration should be manpower. It is difficult for a photographer to walk out alone into a pasture or scenic spot and shoot a top cover photo of cattle, horses, riders, or some related subject. The job requires planning and setting up the shot, and to set it up properly requires the aid of several helpers.

Next, the site should be taken into account. Every area has some natural grandeur, be it snow-capped mountains, moss-draped trees, desert and cactus, or a vast expanse of plain. The wise photographer takes advantage of the very best local scenery, combining it with the subject under the most advantageous light conditions.

A favorite scenic set-up of mine has included a natural frame around, over, or under the main subject. This might be an overhanging tree limb, downed timber, rock bluffs, windmills, dark shadows cast by nearby trees or fences, or any other choice local feature.

If no frame is available, make one. Once, in Michigan, I was shooting a calendar photo for a prominent Appaloosa farm. The subject was brood mares, and I had driven all over the area hunting for an acceptable scenic spot. It was pretty country, but all level pasture, or forest so dense that the sun barely penetrated. The pasture where the mares were kept had no special scenery in any direction. It did have some advantages, however. It was out in the country, so no highways, electric poles, or ice-cream trucks cluttered the background.

Finally, a compromise of available components was reached. Two farm hands were sent to saw off a large, long tree limb. Another hand fixed up a farm tractor with a front end loader. The limb was chained to the loader and driven to a gently rolling hill in a rich, blossoming alfalfa field. A half-dozen riders then drove the brood mares to the field and loosely herded them between the tractor and the farm headquarters, so that a golden-ripe oat field in front of the buildings showed behind the alfalfa.

The tractor's front end loader was tilted up and down until I was satisfied that the tree limb was angled properly to form an attractive frame across the top of the scene. A clear-sky background with a few fluffy clouds added extra appeal. When it was time to snap the photo, the mares were gathered into a central area and held there by horsemen on either side so the entire herd could be pictured, yet no horseman or any part of the front end loader appeared in the final calendar shot.

I cannot boast that this turned out to be a photo of awe-inspiring beauty, but it represented a concentrated effort to present the mares at their best and at the same time make use of — and improve — the local scenery. Of course, a different set of obstacles and a different project would require different solutions, and it is here that an imaginative photographer proves his worth.

There are other limitations besides the scenery in setting up a cover-quality shot. Most magazines require vertical color transparencies in order to fill the usual 8½ x 11 front cover area. A smaller percentage use horizontal cover shots because it is awkward to fill the space above and below such pictures. Therefore, if magazines are your market, plan for a majority of vertical subjects. Most calendar publishers, however, prefer horizontal shots over a vertical format.

The West, in particular, is filled with horizontal country, and this calls for extra effort in putting a vertical shot together. The photographer must search for rough areas with deep canyons and use the canyon walls for sides. Or he can place his main subject low in the photo and make the background extend further into the distance and upward toward the top of the photo. To a photographer with imagination, any number of situations can be arranged that will bunch in the subjects from the sides and extend the background outward and up for vertical action. Often, the telephoto lens helps. It will bring distant objects — a stand of trees or a rocky pinnacle, for example — closer to the main subject and the middle of the scene, thus increasing the vertical effect.

Frequently, a scene must be planned a day in advance to get the proper light angle so that the sun brightens the color to the photographer's satisfaction. For instance, you may envision a beautiful shot looking toward the west. It is four o'clock in the afternoon, however, and the low sun is hitting your subject's top line and far side, revealing only a shadowed front side. Early morning light striking the top and front of the subject would be far superior, so this shot will have to be done early the following day to achieve the most artistic picture. Anything worth doing is worth doing right, even if it involves extra planning, time, and effort.

PHOTOGRAPHING RANCH FACILITIES

PHOTOS OF RANCH FACILITIES are used for advertising accommodations for boarding horses, ranches for sale, and to show the taste and competence of the ranch owner. Many people judge a ranch owner's character and general ability by the condition of his property and whether it is well or poorly maintained.

The first place to look for an eye-catching shot is from the road approaching the property. The approach to a ranch, often with a high gate and a sign with the name of the spread, is generally the most visually attractive part of the property and the best place for pictures. A variety of angles should be considered to fully capture whatever eye-appeal there may be. If necessary, a wide-angle 28mm lens can be used to push the background away. A 200mm telephoto lens from a nearby hillside will bring the background up closer.

Here is another situation where a well-chosen frame can add interest to a picture. To frame the main house or a horse-training arena, try the ranch's main entrance gate or an overhanging tree limb. Also, try to combine some spot of scenery, such as a flower bed or a clump of trees, with a photo of a building. Barns are especially bare-looking, but a touch of natural beauty can turn a picture of an ordinary barn into a work of art.

Having livestock in the photos of ranch facilities adds life to the pictures. If the foreground is a pasture, have feed distributed in one area so the animals will congregate there. Try to emphasize the most outstanding animal in the herd as the featured one. If the shot shows white rail fences and roads, have someone lead a horse by the fence or move a group of cattle down the road.

If you are shooting the hallway of a barn or shed row, a wide-angle lens will make it look longer and wider, and someone rubbing down a horse's legs

This show-barn hallway reveals the ranch owner's taste and the efficient way he has designed improvements. A wide-angle lens is tops here.

or otherwise grooming him adds a little action. Available light is superior to flash on this shot.

In any ranch facility picture, include as much of the best improvements as possible, but avoid any area that might show poor care. Every ranch needs a trash barrel, but no one needs a close-up of it in an ad.

Occasionally a very large ranch must be photographed from the air to show a number of important facilities (see *Camera Shutter Speeds,* page 3). If you or the ranch owner do not have a plane handy, the nearest local airport may be able to rent you a plane or, better yet, a helicopter.

PHOTOGRAPHING A WORLD CHAMPION WITH A SIMPLE CAMERA

MANY PROCEDURES in this book have emphasized techniques usable only by professional photographers or people with fairly expensive and complex cameras.

If your camera does not fit this category, your photos, may not be as sharp and exciting, but there is hope.

Most simple, inexpensive cameras have only one fixed lens and one non-adjustable shutter speed. The lens is a semi-wide-angle one, usually with a fixed zone of sharp focus — fine for birthday parties, family vacations, or kindergarten graduation pictures. The shutter speed is generally 1/40 or 1/50 second, so the camera must be held very steady to avoid blurs. Nevertheless, it is amazing how versatile these little machines are. Their lens and shutter speed actually give a tremendous latitude for general, all-around photo situations, and they can fill a scrapbook with memories to treasure for a lifetime.

For livestock photography, simple cameras obviously have serious limitations, but good pictures with uncomplicated equipment should not be ruled out as impossible.

First of all, forget front and rear views of animals. The distortion with a wide-angle lens would be tremendous. The side view *will* work, however. Use the same procedures described for weather, light, camera elevation, and positioning the subject, and good photos — sometimes even of advertising quality — can be taken.

Be careful that the subject's head does not turn toward the camera and appear abnormally large to the wide-angle lens. Get in close enough to the subject to fill the picture with the animal, and position yourself fairly close to the side view angle (see *Side View Shots,* page 48). Slightly closer to the animal's rear is better than being directly perpendicular to its spine because it gives the improved effect of a larger hip and smaller head.

A final word of warning: if your camera uses half-inch-square 16mm film, don't expect the negatives to enlarge to a sharp 16 x 20 like the negatives of larger films.

The extent of accomplishment with an economy camera may be limited, but with care and serious effort, the results often can be surprising.

CROPPING THE FINISHED PHOTO

CROPPING A PRINT is the final stage in preparing a picture for its public appearance. Proper cropping is an art in itself. The crop can emphasize fundamental features, or it can waste large areas of a photo.

In snapping a picture, most good photographers allow extra space on both

This bull was not gentled or broken to the halter as a calf. As a mature ton-plus animal, he had to be photographed while tied securely to a tractor loader. This is one of several shots. In the better ones, the man relaxing in the foreground has moved elsewhere, and the bull's muzzle can be seen. For the finished photos, the loader was cropped, and only the bull showed.

---

sides of the main subject just to play around with. This gives room to make the finished print a vertical or a horizontal one.

For livestock, the goal is to emphasize the subject to its fullest, making the animal fill the whole photo area. In an 8 x 10 print, for example, the animal should fill the photo to within ⅜ inch of the margin on sides, top, and bottom. No one made a rule that all photos must be a standard 8 x 10, however. If the subject is long, tall, fat, or skinny, make the print to fit that subject.

Correct cropping should cut out poor background and concentrate on the animal itself. Sometimes a photographer gets carried away by clouds, a white fence, or some pretty trees in the background, and does not crop these extra features. But the cowman is more interested in the bull's structure and could not care less about the clouds. The clouds will not sell that bull or his calves for a premium, but a good photo of the bull alone will.

88

DESIGNED BY ROBERT JACOBSON
COMPOSED IN LINOTYPE GARAMOND
WITH HANDSET COLUMBIA BOLD DISPLAY TYPE

AT THE PRESS IN THE PINES

NORTHLAND PRESS

BOUND BY ROSWELL BOOKBINDING
PHOENIX